IN | PORT LANGUAGES

Ina Pförtner

Placement Test for Occupational German Language Courses

Proficiency assessment based on the Common European Framework of Reference for Languages

Model 1

A1 | A2 | B1 | B2 | C1

IN | PORT®LANGUAGES

ISBN 978-3-9819522-4-7

© IN|PORT® Languages Ina Pförtner, Berlin
Schöneberger Str. 12, 12163 Berlin, Germany
verlag@in-port.de

Design: Dr Oliver Maor
Translation: Dr Oliver Maor
Original language: German

Contribution and Consulting: Kazim Karadag
(SECONOS Qualifications & Services GmbH, Berlin, Germany)

IN|PORT is a name mark registered in the Federal Republic of Germany.

Picture on the title © Rido

IN|PORT LANGUAGES

Preface

Dear provider of language classes,
dear assessment provider,

thank you very much for your confidence in our product. We are grateful for your decision to use this proficiency test, which is specially designed for the assessment of the language skills of scholars in occupational training courses of the German language. As reading and writing skills play a particularly important role on the labor market, this test is focused on the optimum assessment of these skills by checking the vocabulary and the reading skills.

Given this, we have decided to offer a scalable format, which means that the level of difficulty is stepped up with each single exercise. Immediately after the test, you can calculate the result using our scoring sheet at the end of this brochure.

This enables you to perform the grading of all members of even very large groups of students, simplifying the correct placement of participants to the appropriate classes. Furthermore, this placement test allows the easy review of the level of proficiency during a language class.

We wish all participants much success.

IN|PORT LANGUAGES

For instructions, please refer to page 12.

Table of contents

IN|PORT LANGUAGES

Data of the Participant

Given name: _____

Last name: _____

Gender: ☐ male ☐ female

Date of birth: _____

Place of birth: _____

Nationality: _____

Family status: ☐ single ☐ married
☐ children

Address: _____

_____

E-Mail: _____

Telephone number: _____

Profession: _____

For how long have you been learning German:
☐ years

V

Vocabulary

Vocabulary Exercise A1/A2

Exercise 1

In each row, strike out the one word which does not belong:

Example:

werken	arbeiten	~~schlafen~~	sich bemühen
arbeiten	jobben	pausieren	sich bewerben
Spielplatz	Werkstatt	Büro	Arbeitsplatz
pünktlich	verantwortlich	fleißig	müde
teamfähig	kommunikativ	erfahren	kritikresistent

Points: /4

Exercise 2

Form an existing word: Put together the matching parts (draw lines):

Example: Hand + Werk = Handwerk

1. Büro…   x …werk

2. Arbeits…   a …meister

3. Werk…   b …tisch

4. Haus…   c …statt

5. Schreib…   d …stuhl

X. Hand…   e …platz

Points: /5

Exercise 3

Find synonyms (what belongs to each other? – draw double arrows):

Example: unpünktlich ⟷ zu spät

ARBEITEN   **BETRIEB**   **ARBEITSLOS**

ERWERBSLOS   **TÄTIG SEIN**   **ARBEITSSTÄTTE**

Points: /6

2

Vocabulary Exercise B1

Exercise 1

<u>In each row, strike out the one word which does not belong:</u>

vorschlagen	ergänzen	empfehlen	widersprechen
Praktikant	Geldkarte	Kredit	Urlaubsgeld
fachkundig	zusätzlich	eingearbeitet	selbstständig
ausschließlich	nur	lediglich	nebenbei

Points: /4

Exercise 2

<u>Form an existing word: Put together the matching parts (draw lines):</u>

Example: Hand + Werker = Handwerker

X. Hand…   a …kammer

1. Lohn…   b …gespräch

2. Lebens…   c …steuer

3. Handels…   d …lauf

4. Mittel…   e …stand

5. Verkaufs…   x …werker

Points: /5

Exercise 3

<u>Find synonyms (what belongs to each other? – draw double arrows):</u>

Beispiel: kontrollieren ←→ prüfen

ARBEITSBEREICH   **EINE UNIVERSITÄT BESUCHEN**   **NÖTIG**

ERFORDERLICH   **STUDIEREN**   **BRANCHE**

Points: /6

3

Vocabulary Exercise B2

Exercise 1

In each row, strike out the one word which does not belong:

sich beziehen	sich informieren	nachfragen	sich erkundigen
absurd	abgetan	abwegig	unvertretbar
Zuschlag	Skonto	Abzug	Rabatt
binnen	intern	innerhalb	intensiv

Points: /4

Exercise 2

Form an existing word: Put together the matching parts (draw lines):

Example: Hand + Werker = Handwerker

X. Hand…   a …kraft

1. Beschwerde…   b …prozess

2. Pflege…   c …pendler

3. Berufs…   d …schifffahrt

4. Binnen   e …kantine

5. Werks…   x …werker

Points: /5

Exercise 3

Find synonyms (what belongs to each other? – draw double arrows):

Example: kontrollieren ⟷ prüfen

ABWEISEN   SÄMTLICH   GÄNZLICH

WEGBITTEN   VORGESETZER   FÜHRUNGSKRAFT

Points: /6

Vocabulary Exercise C1

Exercise 1

In each row, strike out the one word which does not belong:

untergraben	sabotieren	stören	kontaminieren
verringern	vermindern	vereiteln	verkleinern
Einkommensteuer	Aussteuer	Umsatzsteuer	Lohnsteuer
Des Weiteren	außerdem	ungeachtet	überdies

Points: /4

Exercise 2

Form an existing word: Put together the matching parts (draw lines):

Example: Hand + Werker = Handwerker

X. Hand…   a …fehler

1. Daten   b …diagnose

2. Podiums…   x. …werker

3. Insolvenz…   c …verfahren

4. Fern…   d …diskussion

5. Verfahrens…   e …verarbeitung

Points: /5

Exercise 3

Find synonyms (what belongs to each other? – draw double arrows):

Example: kontrollieren ←→ prüfen

MEINUNGSUMFRAGE   **ABSURD**   **POSTULIEREN**

BEHAUPTEN   **ABWEGIG**   **ERHEBUNG**

Points: /6

Language Modules

Language Modules A1/A2

> Sehr geehrte Frau Müller,
>
> im Internet haben wir __01____ Anzeige gelesen. Dort steht, dass
>
> __02____ Ihr Auto verkaufen __03_____. Da wir uns
>
> __04____ Ihr Angebot interessieren, möchten wir Sie um einen Termin
>
> __05_____. Wir sind in der Automobilbranche als Autohändler tätig und
>
> möchten gerne Ihr Fahrzeug kaufen.

01	a seine	02	a Sie	03	a möchten
	b Ihre		b du		b können
	c deine		c sich		c brauchen

04	a auf	05	a machen	Points: _____ /5
	b für		b geben	
	c an		c bitten	

> Liebe Sara,
>
> leider kann ich morgen nicht zur Arbeit __06____. Ich habe Husten und Schnupfen
> und der Arzt sagt, __07____ ich eine Woche zu Hause bleiben __08____. __09__ich aber
> einen wichtigen Kundentermin habe, brauche ich eine Vertretung. Kannst du mich
> am Montag vertreten? Der Kunde heißt Herr Cabik und ein sehr wichtiger
> Geschäftspartner für __10____.
>
> Könntest du das tun?
>
> Vielen Dank im Voraus für deine Hilfe.
>
> Barbara

06	a kommen	07	a deshalb	08	a brauch
	b kommt		b ob		b muss
	c kömmt		c dass		c will

09	a Deshalb	10	a uns	Points: _____ /5
	b Da		b euch	
	c Damit		c Sie	

Bewerbung 11_____ einen Praktikumsplatz im Bereich Krankenpflege

Sehr geehrte Damen und Herren,

ich habe Ihre Stellenanzeige im Internet 12_____Ihrer Homepage gelesen.

13_____ möchte ich mich auf die ausgeschriebene Stelle bewerben. Ich bin

Krankenpfleger 14_____Beruf und habe 9 Jahre in Kroatien in diesem

15_____ gearbeitet. Dadurch habe ich viel Erfahrung

16_____ der Krankenpflege.

Weil ich auch in Deutschland in der Krankenpflege tätig sein möchte, möchte

ich dieses Praktikum 17_____. Zu meinen Stärken 18_____Belastbarkeit

und Pünktlichkeit. Über eine Einladung zu einem Vorstellungsgespräch

19_____ ich mich freuen.

Mit 20_____ Grüßen

Bozena Malic

Anlagen: Zeugnisse, Lebenslauf

11	a um b in c bei	12	a über b in c auf	13	a Dazu b Damit c Hiermit	14	a von b für c als
15	a Teil b Gebiet c Bereich	16	a in b durch c mit	17	a absolvieren b machten c tun	18	a gehören b zahlen c sind
19	a werde b wurde c würde	20	a freundlicher b freundlichen c freundliche	**Points:**	____/10		

9

IN|PORT®LANGUAGES

Language Modules B2

Letzte Mahnung

Sehr geehrte Frau Mustermann,

nach __21_____ unseres Kundenkontos haben wir festgestellt, dass der folgende Betrag zum Fälligkeitstermin noch nicht beglichen wurde. Trotz mehrmaliger Schreiben an Sie haben wir bislang keinen Zahlungseingang feststellen können. __22_____ Berücksichtigung Ihrer Zahlungseingänge bis zum heutigen Datum erinnern wir Sie __23_____ an die Begleichung unserer Forderung von 5 000 Euro.

Da Sie ein langjähriger und geschätzter Kunde sind, möchten wir auch in Ihrem Interesse weitere Kosten __24_____. Wir hoffen __25_____, Sie auf diesem Weg erreichen zu können und bitte Sie erneut und __26_____ um Ausgleich des Betrags von 5 000 Euro bis zum 30.09.20xx.

Sollten Sie dies nicht tun, sehen wir uns __27_____, die laufende Geschäftsbeziehung zu __28_____ und rechtliche Schritte gegen Sie einzuleiten. Sollten Sie die Zahlung des fälligen Betrages __28_____ vorgenommen haben, können Sie dieses Schreiben selbstverständlich __29_____ gegenstandslos betrachten.

Bei Rückfragen stehen wir selbstverständlich gern zur Verfügung.

Mit freundlichen Grüßen

xxx xxx

---

a ALS	**e** DURCHSICHT	**i** KÜNDIGEN	**m** UNTER
b AN	**f** ERNEUT	**j** LETZTMALIG	**n** VERMEIDEN
c AUSSICHT	**g** GEZWUNGEN	**k** VERLÄNGERN	**o** ZWINGEN
d DAHER	**h** HIERMIT	**l** SCHON	**Points:** ___/10

Mehr Frauen in Führungspositionen

Die Frauenquote wirkt. Das zeigt der Bericht für den Deutschen Bundestag, den das Kabinett 31_____ hat. Es gibt mehr Frauen in Aufsichtsräten, und Unternehmen haben sich 32_____ ambitionierte Ziele gesetzt. Seit Anfang 2016 gilt die Frauenquote für die Wirtschaft und den öffentlichen Dienst.

33_____ der regelmäßigen Information der Öffentlichkeit ist 34___ Gesetz zwei Jahre nach Inkrafttreten ein Bericht an den Deutschen Bundestag vorzulegen. Für das Geschäftsjahr 2015 sind 35_____ alle vom Gesetz erfassten Gesellschaftsformen ausgewertet und liegen als Ergebnis 36_____ .

Seit dem 1. Januar 2016 gilt die feste Geschlechterquote von 30 Prozent 37_____ neu zu besetzende Aufsichtsratsposten in börsennotierten und voll mitbestimmten Unternehmen. Unternehmen, die börsennotiert oder mitbestimmungspflichtig sind, mussten 38_____ bis zum 30. September 2015 erstmals Zielgrößen festlegen. Anderthalb Jahre nach 39_____ des Gesetzes ist in den Aufsichtsräten eine deutliche Steigerung des Frauenanteils zu verzeichnen: In Unternehmen, die 40_____ die feste Quote von 30 Prozent fallen, ist dieser Anteil im Geschäftsjahr 2015 von 25 auf 27,3 Prozent gestiegen.

(Source: www.bundesregierung.de)

31	a geschieden	34	a auf	37	a wegen	40	a unter
	b verabschiedet		b bei		b auf		b auf
	c verschieden		c wegen		c für		c bei
	d bescheinigt		d laut		d von		d mit

32	a niemals	35	a erstmals	38	a abgesehen	**Points:** _____ /10
	b meistens		b erstmaliger		b außerhalb	
	c manchmal		c einmalig		c außerdem	
	d zurzeit		d damalig		d innerhalb	

33	a unter	36	a vor	39	a Ausstaffieren
	b auf		b nach		b Inkrafttreten
	c neben		c auf		c Vorbeugung
	d für		d unter		d Vertreten

How to use this test

1. **No German language skills required for institutional staff** – this test is completely designed to be handled by persons who do not have any German language skills.

2. **The data page (page V)** – that page can be used for collecting some relevant data from participants. The participants can be asked to fill in this form. If you do not require some data, or if you have already collected them otherwise, you can leave it up to the participant to leave items blank.

3. **Taking the exercises** – All participants should be requested to try to perform all exercises in this booklet. As the exercises are scalable, the level of difficulty will increase as they proceed, and some participants might give up at some stage. This is normal, and participants should be allowed to do so. Their language skill level is not assessed upon where they give up, but on the points system explained below.

4. **Design of the exercises** –

    a. **"In each row, strike out the one word which does not belong"** – Each row contains four German words. Three of them have the same, a similar, or a related meaning, or are related to one topic. One word does not share this similarity. For example, in a row containing the English words "work", "labor", "sleep", and "strive", the word "sleep" would fall have to be struck, as it does not refer to a constructive activity.

The participant earns one point for each word which is correctly struck out.

b. **Compound words ("put together the matching parts")** – this test helps assessing the vocabulary skills by using a peculiarity of the German language. Compounds are words composed of two or more words as stems. In English, "girlfriend" or "craftsman" can serve as examples. Although they exist in many other languages, they are exceptionally wide-spread in German. Matching compounds requires knowledge of three words. The participant should match the two words which form a valid compound by linking them with an arrow.

It should be noted that this exercise might confuse excellent speakers, as the German language theoretically allows the composition of any two or more words into a new single word. In each exercise, other combinations than those stated in the scoring sheet could lead to exotic, albeit existing words. Nevertheless, not all half words could be matched after "using up" one for exotic combinations. Regular learners of German would only match the most common combination which forms part of the everyday language.

The participant earns one point for each correctly composed word.

c. Find synonyms – The participant should find couples of words or phrases which have about or exactly the same meaning. An English example would be the words "unemployed" and "jobless". The two words forming such a couple should be linked to each other with a double error.

The participant earns two points for every correctly formed couple of words.

d. Cloze test (text with gaps) – The cloze test consists of texts which have gaps, indicated by a number and a line. In the tests for the language skill levels A1/A2 and C1, each number shows up again below the text, together with three or four possible solutions for words filling the related gap. Each of these solutions is combined with a small character (a, b, c, or d). The character of the correct solution should be filled into the gap. In the B2 test, the 10 words which should be filled into the text should be chosen from the 15 words contained in the box below the text. Also here, the small character next to the word chosen should be filled into the gap.

The participant earns one point for each correctly filled gap.

5. Assessment and scoring – The assessment is very easy, using the score sheet at the end of each test.

- One correctly struck out word
  (part "vocabulary", exercise 1):   One point.

- Two words correctly
  matched to a compound
  (part "vocabulary", exercise 2):   One point.

- Two words correctly
  matched as synonyms
  (part "vocabulary", exercise 3):   Two points.

- One word correctly
  matched with a gap
  (part "language modules")   One point.

Add all points. The language skill level can then be assessed using the chart at the end of the score sheet (page 18).

6. **Do not produce photocopies of this brochure, so use one test issue for each participant** – This is not a mere request, but a legal requirement. Copying this test without the prior express consent of the publisher is not only discouraged, but simply illegal.

Score sheet

Vocabulary:

A1/A2:

Exercise 1: pausieren, Spielplatz, müde, kritikresistent

Exercise 2: 1d; 2e; 3c; 4a; 5b

Exercise 3: arbeiten-tätig sein/Betrieb-Arbeitsstätte/arbeitslos-erwerbslos

B1:

Exercise 1: widersprechen, Praktikant, zusätzlich, nebenbei

Exercise 2: 1c; 2d; 3a; 4e; 5b

Exercise 3: Arbeitsbereich-Branche/eine Universität besuchen-studieren/nötig-erforderlich

B2:

Exercise 1: sich beziehen, abgetan, Zuschlag, intensiv

Exercise 2: 1b; 2a; 3c; 4d; 5e

Exercise 3: abweisen-wegbitten/sämtlich-gänzlich/Vorgesetzter-Führungskraft

C1:

Exercise 1: kontaminieren, vereiteln, Aussteuer, ungeachtet

Exercise 2: 1e; 2d; 3c; 4b; 5a

Exercise 3: Meinungsumfrage-Erhebung/absurd-abwegig/postulieren-behaupten

Language Modules:

A1/A2:	B1:	B2:	C1:
01) b	11) a	21) e	31) b
02) a	12) c	22) m	32) d
03) a	13) c	23) f	33) c
04) b	14) a	24) n	34) d
05) c	15) c	25) d	35) a
06) a	16) a	26) j	36) a
07) c	17) a	27) g	37) c
08) b	18) a	28) l	38) c
09) b	19) c	29) a	39) b
10) a	20) b	30) k	40) a

Scoring

Points	Level
Less than 15	A1 or below
16 to 25	A2
26 to 51	B1
52 to 77	B2
78 to 100	C1